Gray Wolves

by Grace Hansen

Peachtree

Abdo Kids
ANIMALS OF NORTH AMERICA

abdopublishing.com

Published by Abdo Kids, a division of ABDO, PO Box 398166, Minneapolis, Minnesota 55439.

Printed in the United States of America, North Mankato, Minnesota.

102015

012016

THIS BOOK CONTAINS RECYCLED MATERIALS

Photo Credits: iStock, Shutterstock

Production Contributors: Teddy Borth, Jennie Forsberg, Grace Hansen

Design Contributors: Laura Mitchell, Dorothy Toth

Library of Congress Control Number: 2015941771

Cataloging-in-Publication Data

Hansen, Grace.

Gray wolves / Grace Hansen.

p. cm. -- (Animals of North America)

ISBN 978-1-68080-110-1 (lib. bdg.)

Includes index.

1. Gray wolf--Juvenile literature. 2. Wolves--Juvenile literature. I. Title.

599.773--dc23

2015941771

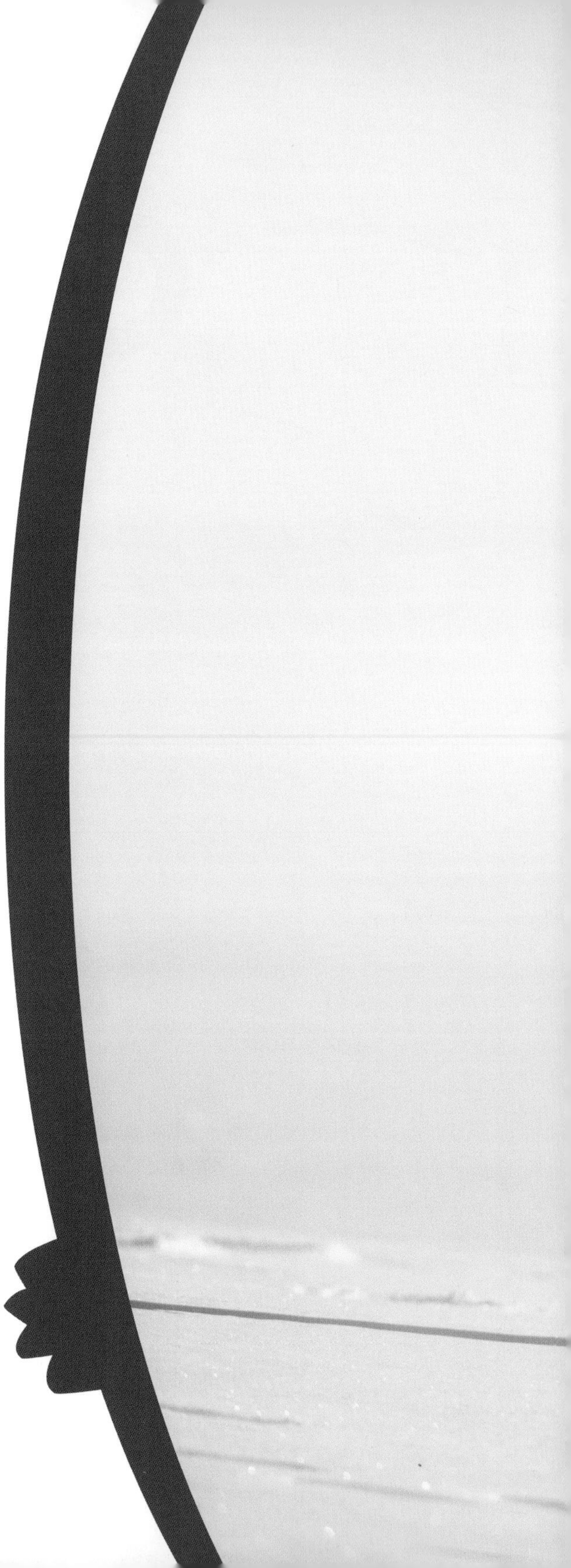

Table of Contents

Gray Wolves

Gray Wolves live in North America. They also live in Europe and Asia.

Gray wolves live in many **habitats**. They live in forests and deserts. They live in woodlands, too.

A gray wolf's fur is often many colors. It is gray, black, tan, and brown. Some gray wolves are all white!

Gray wolves have bushy tails.

They have large, upright ears.

Wolf Packs

Gray wolves are **social** animals. They live and hunt in packs. Each pack usually has 6 to 10 wolves.

Packs work together to catch **prey**. They eat deer, elk, and moose. They eat smaller mammals, too. They also like fish, reptiles, and fruit.

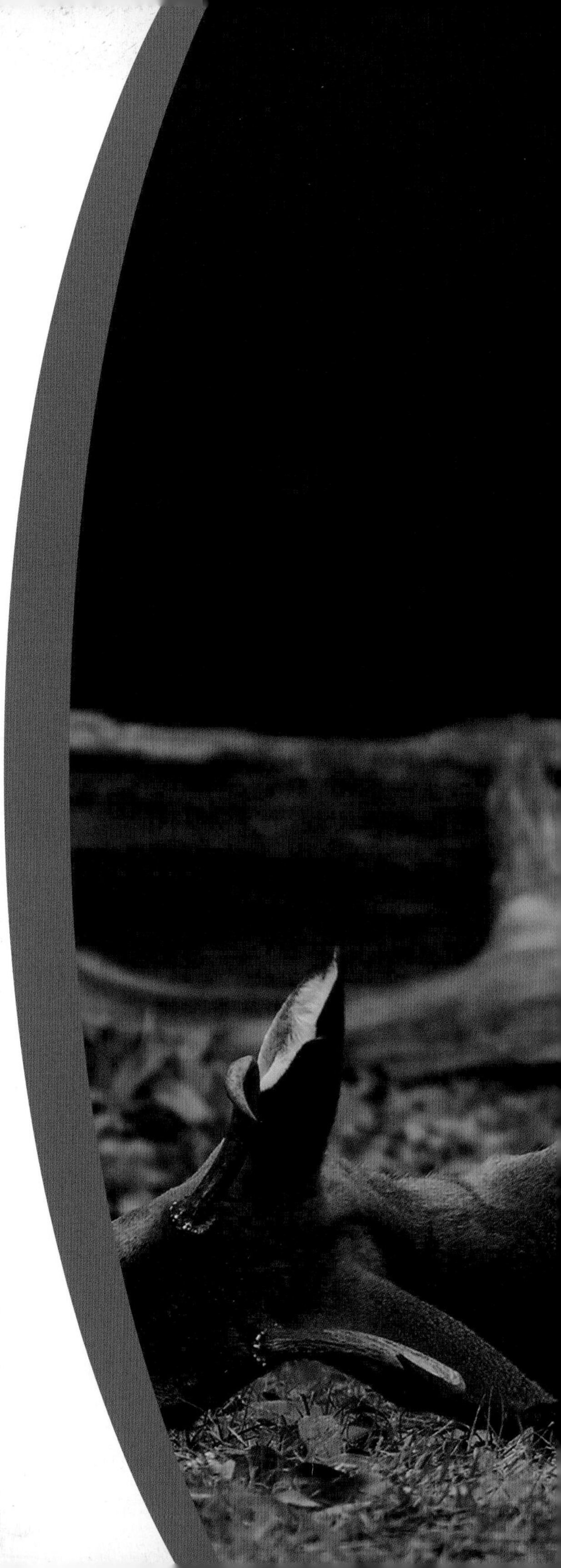

One male leads each pack. A female also leads the pack. The male and female are called the alpha pair. These two are often the only wolves to have pups.

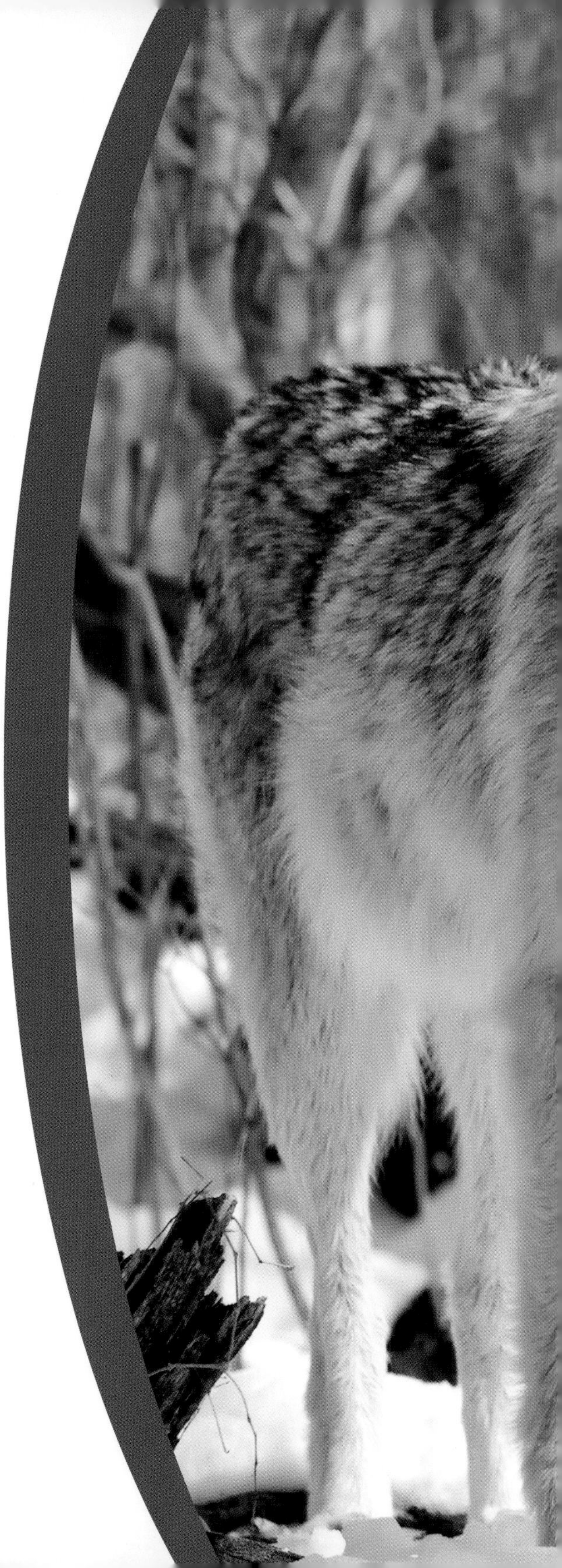

Baby Gray Wolves

A wolf **litter** usually has 4 to 7 pups. The pups are born in a **den**. The den keeps them safe and warm. They stay in their den for about 6 weeks.

The pack cares for the pups. Pups can hunt at about 10 months old. Soon, they might leave to join new packs.

More Facts

- Gray wolves howl to communicate.

- Each wolf has a unique howl. A howl is like a person's fingerprints. No two are the same. Other wolves know exactly who is calling!

- A wolf can eat 20 pounds (9 kg) of meat at one meal!

Glossary

den – an animal's home that is often underground or on the side of a hill.

habitat – a place where an animal naturally and normally lives.

litter – all of the pups born at one time to a mother wolf.

prey – an animal hunted or killed by a predator for food.

social – naturally living or growing in groups, rather than alone.

Index

abdokids.com

Use this code to log on to abdokids.com and access crafts, games, videos, and more!

Abdo Kids Code: AGK1101